2021-2022

Horse Riding in Every State & Country

KRYSTAL KELLY

D1664438

For all the equestrian adventuresses with wandering hearts and restless feet...

Preface
Welcome to the Equestrian Adventuresses Tribe!

Thank you for being a part of this wonderful adventure. Welcome to the Equestrian Adventuresses Travel Guide Book Series.

We have worked hard to dig deep and find the top horse riding destinations around the world for you to book your next horse riding expedition. We update the information in this Travel Guide Series every year so please make sure you have downloaded the most recent edition. You can find out more on our website: www.equestrianadventuresses.com

If you are the owner of a riding stable or holiday destination and are not on this list and would like to be featured in next years catalog please get in touch with us.

If you book a riding holiday or use any of the stables in this directory, please share your feedback, photos and stories with us! You may email us on our website or join our Facebook Group - Equestrian Adventuresses to let other adventuresses know that you enjoyed your experience!

Last year's Travel Guide Books were well received by our Equestrian Adventuresses Community. Because of the series, countless horse riders around the world have traveled and ridden at some pretty spectacular places such as Dubai, Croatia, Bosnia and Herzegovina and even Rwanda!

The Horse Riding in Every Country Catalog was designed to be like a phone-book directory for quick reference. You'd be surprised that even with the internet and resources like "Trip Advisor" how difficult it can be to find quality horse riding stables around the world that don't just cater to tourists or beginners! That is why this book came into fruition, the first of the series nearly 3 years ago.

This book is there for you each and every time you get the urge to ride off into the sunset in a new destination and has brought our tribe of adventuresses together to ride Marwari horses in India, race across the beaches of France, tolt on an Icelandic and so much more.

It has been a real blessing watching the friendships formed in the Equestrian Adventuresses community so be sure to head over to our Facebook Group and introduce yourself. You never know where you might end up and the kind of friends you will make for life.

"My heart belongs to the arena but my soul belongs to the trail." -Anonymous

Yours Truly, Krystal Kelly

Founder of Equestrian Adventuresses
www.EquestrianAdventuresses.com

Other Books By Equestrian Adventuresses:

EQUESTRIAN ADVENTURESSES SERIES

Book 1: Saddles and Sisterhood
Book 2: Going the Distance
Book 3: Leg Up
Book 4: Have Breeches Will Travel
Book 5: Horse Nomads

TRAVEL GUIDE FOR EQUESTRIANS SERIES

Best in 2020 World Travel Guide
Best in 2020 USA Travel Guide
2021 Job Book - How to Work Abroad with Horses
Horse Riding in Every State & Country

*Download your FREE E-Book here:
www.EquestrianAdventuresses.com

Coming Soon!

Around the World on 180 Horses Series
Fairy Tail

*Books are available on Amazon, Audible, Kobo and more!
You can also find them on our website:
www.equestrianadventuresses.com

About
Equestrian Adventuresses

Equestrian Adventuresses was founded in 2019 as a community for women who love horses, travel and adventure. Their mission has been clear from the start: to help empower women around the world and be able to provide them with the tools and resources they need to have adventures on horseback whether it be long riding across the Americas, booking a horse riding vacation, or setting off into the sunset on your own horse.

You can listen to more inspirational stories from real women's travels on horseback on the podcast show available on iTunes, Spotify, Stitcher and more. http:bit.lyeqa-podcast

You can also find a variety of travel documentaries on the Youtube Channel:
www.youtube.com/c/equestrianadventuresses

You can also read short stories and find helpful resources on the website:
www.equestrianadventuresses.com

Join the community and check out the Facebook Group:
https:www.facebook.com/groups/equestrianadventuresses

Disclaimer

Although we did our best to include relevant horse riding stables for experienced riders, it is simply impossible for us to physically visit each and every stables in the world in order to verify them.

Please use caution when booking any horse riding expedition without doing the proper research and vetting of the people, horse care and accommodations. It is your responsibility to look at their website's thoroughly, check the reviews, and post in our Facebook Group: Equestrian Adventuresses if you are looking to see photos and hear firsthand reviews of the destination you're interested to visit.

I've always believed in transparency and so I am disclosing that I've included certain links to booking sites that I will earn an affiliate commission for any purchases you make—at no extra cost to you. Please note that I have not been given any free products or services by these companies in exchange for mentioning them. The only consideration is in the form of affiliate commissions or compensation for advertising.

If you have any questions regarding the above, don't hesitate to reach out to us on our website:

www.equestrianadventuresses.com

Interested in traveling the world on horseback but don't know if you are a confident enough rider?

In the Speaking the Horse Language online course you will learn:

1) How to communicate with horses effectively in the saddle and on the ground in order to travel and ride confidently, even if it's a horse you've never ridden before or in a different type of saddle than you're used to riding.

2) Practical exercises to practice with your horse at home

3) Play games with your horse to get them engaged and more confident

4) Master your body language and energy

5) Build confidence

6) Have fun with your horses and earn their trust!

7) Be able to work with young or spooky horses confidently

8) Problem solve

9) Psychotherapy - many might think you're able to "read horses minds" and do horse telepathy! But there's no magic tricks here, you will learn the tools to simply know what your horse is thinking!

And more!

For more information about the Speaking the Horse Language Online Course click here or visit:
https:catalog.equestrianadventuresses.com/shl-course

Are you stressed or worried about your safety as a solo female traveler?

In the Women's Travel Safety Online Course you will learn:

1) Dress Code for different cultures around the world

2) Inside the Mind of a Criminal (With Guest Instructor Sandra Kelly, a retired Law Enforcement Agent specializing in working with criminals, sex offenders, and rapists.)

3) Transportation and Accommodation safety

4) Periods, Sex, Birth Control and Men (How To's for every culture)

5) The #1 Skill that could SAVE YOUR LIFE

You're also going to get this **BONUS**:

-Complete Access to our Travel Scams 101 Course

This teaches you how to spot the difference between a scam and a con-man versus a friendly person and an unusual circumstance.

You will learn about:

1) The Mafia... not just in Sicily!

2) The stolen motorcycle scam

3) The western union scam

4) The dangers of "voluntourism"

And many others!

As a special bonus you will also get a BONUS VIDEO of Krystal in Russia documenting what she did to escape a car of men that tried to follow her to her hostel.

For more information about the Women's Travel Safety Online Course here or visit:

https:catalog.equestrianadventuresses.com/wts

Table of Contents

Featured Stables Index

(Alphabetical Order)

Featured Travel Agencies Index

Every Country in the World Index

Every State in the USA Index

Worldwide Travel Agencies Index

Resources for Equestrians

Job Listings

How to Use this Book

Throughout this guide book you will find several "badges" on the listings of stables. These badges help you to find the most suitable riding destination quickly based on your preferences, budget, experience and wish-list.

VERIFIED BADGE

A Verified Badge is only given to stables which the Equestrian Adventuresses Team has personally visited and verified the welfare of the horses with their own eyes.

Travel Badges Key:

Budget Badges:

Tours for $1,000 or Less

Tours between $1,000 - $3,000

Tours between $3,000 - $5,000

Luxury Tours $5,000+

Best Time of the Year to Visit:

 All Year   Nov-Feb   Mar-Oct   June-July

Travel Badges Key: (Continued)

Topography:

Mountains

Forests

Beaches

Jungle

Deserts

Meadows

Historical Sites

Rivers / Lakes

Villages

Riding Experience:

Beginners   Intermediate   Experienced   Non-Riders Welcome

Pace of Riding:

Mostly Walking

Variety

Fast Riding

Time in Saddle Per Day:

 1-3 hours   3-5 hours   5+ hours   variety

Travel Badges Key: (Continued)

Weather:

Sunshine   Humid   Rain   Snow   Plan for Anything

Ridng Disciplines:

English   Western   Show Jumping   Endurance

Dressage   Polo   Natural Horsemanship

DISCOVER OMAN

Happytravelsoman

WWW.HAPPYTRAVELSOMAN.COM

Brushy Creek
Outdoor Adventures
573-269-4600

GPS Address:
420 County Road 831
Black, MO. 63625

Mailing Address:
5910 Hwy J
Black, MO. 63625

www.brushycreeklodge.com
info@brushycreeklodge.com

imagine riding

www.imagineriding.com

BIG SKY RANCH
NICARAGUA

Beach Rides
Mountain Rides
Full Moon Rides
Monkey Viewing Rides

discover Nicaragua
on horseback

www.bigskyranchnicaragua.com

Costa Rica

Casagua Horses & the Painted Pony Guest Ranch

Join us for a day ride or stay with us on the ranch for a real Adventure in Paradise. The Painted Pony is a family owned guest ranch minutes from Costa Rica's Pacific beaches. From complete riding vacation packages from 3 to 14 days, to a variety of 2 to 5 hour day horseback tours, our rides are perfect for Adventureses of all ages. From lessons, centered riding and natural horsemanship training to private and small group clinics, we are a complete equestrian center. We love our horses and have a variety of well trained horses for beginners to professional equestrians.

http://www.paintedponyguestranch.com
http://www.casaguahorses.net
info@paintedponyguestranch.com

Casagua Horses & the Painted Pony Guest Ranch:

Nov-Sept

1-3 hours   3-5 hours   5+ hours   variety

Beginners   Experienced

Intermediate   Non-Riders
                      Welcome

English   Western   Show Jumping   Endurance

Dressage   Polo   Natural
                                Horsemanship

Types of Horses Used:

English, Western, Spanish, Dressage, Natural Horsemanship,
Centered/Focused Riding, Working Equitation

Ecuador

imagine riding

www.imagineriding.com

www.imagineriding.com

Imagine Riding

Imagine Riding is offering a one-of-a-kind experience in Ecuador. Not only will we ride with Chagra cowboys in the Ecuadorian Highlands but
we will also follow their work as they roundup their livestock and share with us their lifestyle,
traditions and horsemanship.

Luis Fabini, who has spent decades photographing the horsemen of South America will co-host this ride with our outfitter Gabriel Espinosa and help us access the people and cultural life in a quiet and respectful way. There will also be opportunities to work on your photography skills as well.

Our hosts, together with the Chagras, will guide you through the mountains and valleys of the Ecuadorian highlands. Riding home-bred trekking horses we move from point to point staying in remote working haciendas. From the subtropical montagne Cloud Forests we head towards higher altitude with its rocky volcanic landscapes, passing volcanoes and climbing mountain ridges. Switching from the eastern to the western Andes we ride through rolling hills covered in high altitude fauna endemic to these mountains.

You will travel into the very heart of the Ecuadorian highlands providing the opportunity to immerse yourself in the culture and traditions of the Chagra.

Contact us to find out more.

www.imagineriding.com
imagineriding1@gmail.com

Imagine Horse Riding:

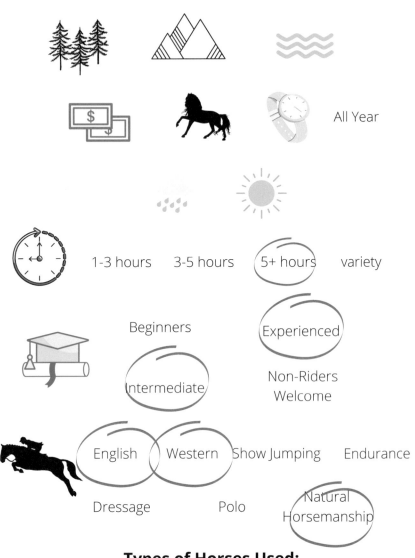

All Year

1-3 hours   3-5 hours   5+ hours   variety

Beginners   Experienced

Intermediate   Non-Riders
Welcome

English   Western   Show Jumping   Endurance

Dressage   Polo   Natural
Horsemanship

Types of Horses Used:

Criollo, Paso, mixed breeds

Ride Andes

Since 1996 Ride Andes has been offering exceptional journeys aboard happy, healthy horses in the Ecuadorian Andes.

Explore Ecuador's staggering geographical diversity - along ancient Inca trails and over mountain passes. Discover snow-capped volcanoes, infinite landscapes and strong indigenous traditions ending each day at a delightful and unique lodge in exquisite scenery.

As Ecuador's leading riding specialist, choose from a comprehensive range of hand-crafted itineraries for every budget and riding ability. From private rides to small group tours to solo safaris, ride with local horsemen and Sally, a horsewoman who has made Ecuador her home for 25 years.

Shirley (Gaucho Derby Pioneer 2020) remarked "Even if you've ridden around the world, as I have, my heart soars at the prospect of returning to ride with Sally in Ecuador. The experience easily stands up to comparison with the better known 'bucket list' destinations. You really need to go and see that for yourself."

Visit www.rideandes.com
Email: rideandes@rideandes.com
Tel/Whatsapp: +593 999 738 221

Ride Andes:

All Year Round

1-3 hours   3-5 hours   5+ hours   variety

Beginners   Experienced

Intermediate   Non-Riders Welcome

English   Western   Show Jumping   Endurance

Dressage   Polo   Natural Horsemanship

Types of Horses Used:

Here in Ecuador we ride horses known as 'improved creoles'- developed over the centuries now crossed with Spanish (PRE), English thoroughbreds, Colombian and Peruvian Pasos. 14.2-15.3hh, responsive yet calm

EGYPT

Equestrian Dream Egypt

We are a stable owned and completely managed by Italians, situated in a very picturesque location surrounded by sand and mountains. The Location and decades of experience enable us to offer different adventures: From "First approach," to the classic riding lessons (English riding), Horsemanship Clinics as well as excursions/tours to the desert.

We organize excursions from 1 hr and full day rides, and you will try the thrill of riding typical Egyptian Horses, quite but always ready to fly like the wind. All our horses are rescued and all retrained following the principle of Natural Horsemanship.

The stable is managed in European Style with a special attention to safety. This is one of the reasons why all our activities are designed custom-made to suit the clients needs.
  Possibility to organize week of RIDE & DIVE!

info@equestriandreamegypt.com
www.equestriandreamegypt.com

Equestrian Dream Egypt:

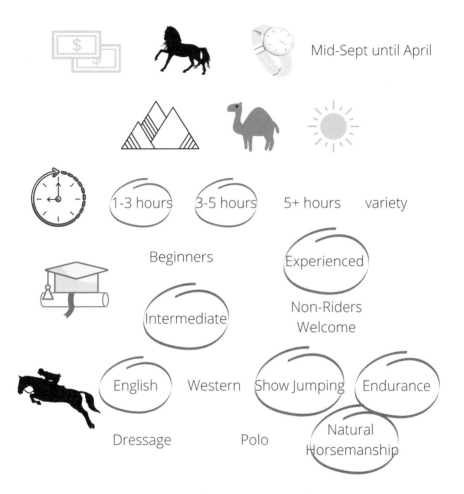

Mid-Sept until April

1-3 hours 3-5 hours 5+ hours variety

Beginners Experienced

Intermediate Non-Riders Welcome

English Western Show Jumping Endurance

Dressage Polo Natural Horsemanship

Types of Horses Used:

Egyptian Horses mostly. Hot blood, and few quite horses. as you may know Egyptian horses are quite small and for this reason we have a weight limit of 90 kgs and height limit of 190cm.

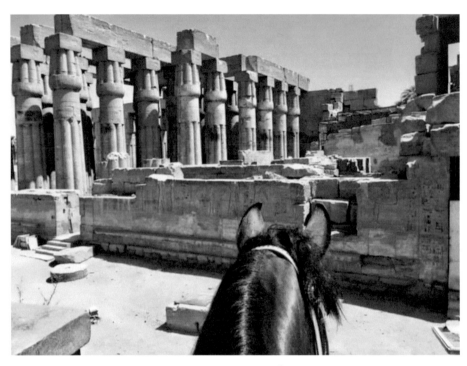

www.imagineriding.com

Imagine Riding

Luxor: this is where you will see the many fabled temples and tombs scattered along the banks of the Nile. It is also where you will ride a swift and elegant Arabian horse through every terrain, from lush sugar plantations and banana groves to palm-fringed lanes and open desert plains. You will discover a simple and peaceful place where traditional feluccas still sail quietly back and forth along the river.

We want to take you a little deeper. Our host, very invested in the community, will invite us into the world of her family and friends. Sharing the food, the music, the customs and the traditions of rural Egypt you may even, in the process of making a new friend, come away having learned how to bake a loaf of bread!
All this against the backdrop of the astonishing 'open-air-musem' of Luxor.

November 13-20, 2021.
Egypt is open for travel with a negative COVID test.
Refundable deposits if related to Covid or possibility to apply the deposit to a later date.

www.imagineriding.com
imagineriding1@gmail.com

France

Read our Stories or Listen to the Audio Books about Riding Across France at age 60 by Equestrian Adventuresses on:

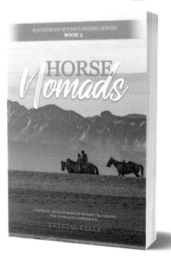

www.EquestrianAdventuresses.com

www.frenchalps-horseridingholidays.com

www.frenchalps-horseridingholidays.com

Ride in the Alps with French Alps Horse Riding

Ride in the french alps is an unique experience, we are located between Chamonix and Geneva, our ride program called " Seven peaks ride" is taking place in Samoens wich mean the 7 peaks village!

The town carries the designation of a "ville fleurie" distinguishing it as one of the most beautiful towns in France.

Approximately a 70 km drive from Geneva Airport, Samoens is a popular summer destination as well as the site of a ski resort that departs from a new lift (Grand massif Express) at the edge of town linking up to Samoëns 1600 also known as the Plateau des Saix, this resort is part of the larger five-town Grand Massif which includes Flaine andMorillon.
Samoëns has been awarded the 'Famille Plus Montagne' label, making it a great destination for a family ski holiday.

Samoëns is the only winter sports resort to be classified by the Caisse Nationale des Monuments Historiques.

We are riding Six Days between Mountains and valleys covering around 150 km of mountain tracks, enjoying Mont Blanc Scenery, fresh air, french cheese and our local beverages !!

This ride do not need a high riding level, but good physical condition. Tracks are safe but we are mostly in Mountains uip 1000 Meters.

Rideinthealps@gmail.com
www.frenchalps-horseridingholidays.com

French Alps Horse Riding:

June-Sept

1-3 hours   3-5 hours   5+ hours   variety

Beginners

Experienced

Intermediate

Non-Riders
Welcome

English   Western   Show Jumping   Endurance

Dressage   Polo   Natural
Horsemanship

Types of Horses Used:

French Riding Holidays

Over 15 years of experience with guests from around the world, riding through the Aveyron and Lot Valley in SW France. We offer the opportunity to ride through enchanting villages, unspoilt woodland, following river valleys and gorges, and canter across fields. We have 26 horses, a variety of breeds, some home bred, to cover different weights, experience and confidence. All the rides have beautiful views and lovely canters. Accommodation is in a traditional Gite just for holiday guests, with 4 separate rooms with ensuite bathrooms, and the original Farmhouse. All meals and picnics for day rides are provided. Arrival on any day and stay as long as you wish. Full inclusive holiday for all riding, accommodation, meals, wines, beers, drinks. We ride 5-6 hours every day. Show jumping paddock and Xcountry course on site
We are open all year round including Christmas and New Year
Great for families. No single supplement. Free Wifi. Outdoor swimming pool and plenty of free parking. 5 or 7 day Trail rides organized for certain weeks.

Email info@frenchridingholidays.co.uk
Website www.frenchridingholidays.co.uk

French Riding Holidays:

All Year Round

1-3 hours   3-5 hours   5+ hours   variety

Beginners   Experienced

Intermediate   Non-Riders Welcome

English   Western   Show Jumping   Endurance

Dressage   Polo   Natural Horsemanship

Types of Horses Used:

Arab, Anglo Arab, Spanish, Appaloosa, Cob, Thoroughbred, Merens, Various Xbreeds, and some homebred.

Greece

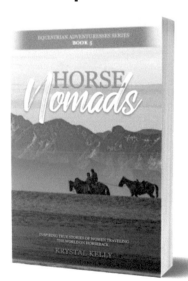

Horseland

At Horseland we provide our clients with a memorable riding experience on one of the most beautiful islands in the Cyclades. We offer the opportunity to discover rural mountains on horseback, riding through breath-taking scenery on the island of Mykonos to a beach off the beaten track. We combine the best of Western and English riding styles, with the ease of soft English reigns and the comfort of the Western saddle. Riders are accompanied by a professional guide to ensure a relaxed and enjoyable experience. Each riding tour starts from the Horseland ranch, and reaches the beach for a ride through the water. A short lesson will commence the trip for beginners. We ride through local farming areas surrounded by rocky mountains, often inhabited by goats, sheep and donkeys. We stop at the stunning beach to take photos, or enjoy a break for lunch and a swim. We offer the option of a private chef a professional photographer, and even live music, as well as a very special romantic evening ride for couples looking to enjoy a truly enchanting and unforgettable Bedouin style experience, complete with fireplace, champagne and the stars above.

mykonoshorseland@hotmail.com
https://mykonoshorse.com
https://www.mykonoshorseriding.com

Horseland:

April - Oct

1-3 hours   3-5 hours   5+ hours   variety

Beginners   Experienced

Intermediate   Non-Riders
                Welcome

English   Western   Show Jumping   Endurance

Dressage   Polo   Natural
                            Horsemanship

Types of Horses Used:

 www.ipposmolyvos.com

Ippos Molyvos

Ippos is a small authentic riding school in Molyvos-Lesvos that has kind and trustworthy horses. We offer you the unique op aportunity to explore the surroundings of Molyvos on horse back and to discover the amazing scenery of rocky mountains and the sandy beaches.

The yard was opened in March 2012 and is located at the heart of Molyvos Village, Lesvos, Greece. Come a get the an authentic Greek lifestyle experience like no other, we have a great combination of horse riding and proper holidays as the yard is situated close to the lovely village of Molyvos, a perfect vacation for the whole family and great for single riders too as we as a yard and the whole region is very welcoming, proper 'filoxenia' a Greek word that translated friend to strangers. Molyvos is a hidden gem, it is a touristic village but not known enough to be crowded, very safe as we are a small community, the food is amazing and our sea is so crystal clean.

There is something beautiful in this village that gives you a sense of relaxation. The hospitality and the laid back lifestyle of the locals pulls you in to join them and if that doesn't do it you can always go to the thermal baths to soak your body in natural warm waters. Otherwise you could have a lazy day at the beach taking in the colourful sunset as it unites with the endless Aegean Sea. Spending your time in Molyvos will help you forget that you ever had problems in your life and most likely you will want to come back for more.

www.ipposmolyvos.com
www.facebook.com/ipposmolyvos
www.instagram.com/ipposmolyvos
www.tiktok.com/ipposmolyvos

Ippos Molyvos:

Spring & Autumn

1-3 hours   3-5 hours   5+ hours   variety

Beginners

Experienced

Intermediate

Non-Riders Welcome

English   Western   Show Jumping   Endurance

Dressage   Polo   Natural Horsemanship

Types of Horses Used:

Halflinger, & Various Mixed breeds. Western saddles available upon request.

Greenland

Riding Greenland

Day 1 Arrival to Narsarsuaq Airport, bus- and boat transfer to Inneruulalik farm. Day 2 Introductory ride nearby the farm area, the entire ride is about 10km. Day 3 Ride to village Qassiarsuk and see norseruins. Ride continues to Tasiusaq farm, the entire ride is about 14km. Day 4 Ride along beach and to the nearby glacier, the entire ride is about 10km. Day 5 Ride back to Inneruulalik farm. Day 6 Boat trip to nearby glacier. Day 7 Ride nearby farm, the entire ride is about 30km. Day 8 Boat- and bus transfer to Narsarsuaq Airport. Breakfast and lunch will be put ready at the hostels. The guests prepare their own lunch pack before the rides. Dinner will be served by the hosts at the farmhouses. The trails are on mountains and can be high up and down. We follow the road of rocks and sometimes go on the sheep trails. There will be no herd of horses with the group, only the horses for the 6 guests and 2 guides. Each guest will ride the same horse every day. Only if the entire group agrees the ride can go on gallop, otherwise the speed won't be fast.

inneruulalik@gmail.com
http://www.riding-greenland.com

Riding Greenland:

    July-August

 1-3 hours 3-5 hours 5+ hours variety

Beginners

Experienced

Intermediate

Non-Riders Welcome

 English Western Show Jumping Endurance

Dressage Polo Natural Horsemanship

Types of Horses Used:

Icelandic horses, expect to ride tolt

India

Horse India

Ride the unique Marwari horse breed of Rajasthan in their homeland. For those with a spirit of adventure wishing to discover fairs & festivals, lakes & leopards, forts & palaces, and the desert dunes of the Great Thar Desert.

You can join our date specific group rides of 7,10,14 days duration, or our 'anytime' private rides. Situated equidistant between the blue city of Jodhpur, the lake city of Udaipur, within easy reach of the pink city of Jaipur. Book now and make it happen!   We look forward to welcoming you on safari with Horse India!

www.horseindia.com
info@horseindia.com

Horse India:

Oct-March (Winter)

1-3 hours   3-5 hours   5+ hours   variety

Beginners   Experienced

Intermediate   Non-Riders Welcome

English   Western   Show Jumping   Endurance

Dressage   Polo   Natural Horsemanship

Types of Horses Used:

Marwari Breed - This breed is a hot blooded breed with great staminia and adorable ears.

www.imagineriding.com

Imagine Riding

This ride was specifically developed for Imagine Riding. The place is Malwa, South-East Rajasthan: lush fields, dotted with villages, small palaces, old hill forts and beautifully adorned farmhouses.

A region traditional in character and appearance and undisturbed by tourism, it is also a pleasure for riders with its softer, level ground perfectly suited for long trots and canters. We visit Boheda, the ancestral village of our guide's family where you can meet some of their friends and family and learn about village life. On two nights we camp on lakeshores full of bird life. We visit the Sita-Mata Wildlife Sanctuary, one of the last virgin forests of Rajasthan home to flying squirrel, spotted deer, sloth bear and leopard.
The ride takes place during Navratri, a nine-day festival devoted to the worship of Goddess Durga. We will be able to take part in local festivities.

The ride culminates with the Ashwa Pooja in the City Palace of Udaipur. This colorful, age-old traditional ceremony honors the horse as a symbol of strength and royalty. An unforgettable comfortable camping trip with the last two nights spent in a historic heritage hotel.

06.10-15.10.2021
26.09. - 05.10.2022
15.10. - 24.10.2023

www.imagineriding.com
imagineriding1@gmail.com

Imagine Horse Riding:

Oct - Feb

1-3 hours   3-5 hours   5+ hours   variety

Beginners   Experienced

Intermediate   Non-Riders Welcome

English   Western   Show Jumping   Endurance

Dressage   Polo   Natural Horsemanship

Types of Horses Used:

Marwari

Princess Trails

Discover Rajasthan on Horseback!

Ride on the back of naturally-trained Marwari horses which are a pleasure to ride, responsive and unique. Every horse is a family member to us and many were born on our farm and brought up by us. We use comfortable trail saddles with endurance stirrups to maximise comfort and safety of horse and rider. Ride with us through rural Rajasthan, away from the crowds, through its countless villages and fascinating landscapes of mountains, plains and deserts. Encounter its many different people, its ancient culture and heritage and stay as a guest and friend rather than just a tourist! Gallop windswept plains or cross the rugged Aravalli Mountains on the back of our sure-footed and comfortable horses who will carry you tirelessly to places not accessible by car or other forms of transport. Together we will show you the heart of Rajasthan, its unique wildlife, nature and its many hidden gems. Stay overnight in Heritage Hotels, often ancient palaces or hunting lodges or in our comfortable safari camp in the Indian bush and dine under the stars! Besides horse safaris we also organise stationary rides and horsemanship lessons with Marwari horses. A unique equestrian adventure awaits you!

marwarihorses@web.de
www.princesstrails.com

Princess Trails:

Nov-March

1-3 hours   3-5 hours   5+ hours   variety

Beginners

Experienced

Intermediate

Non-Riders Welcome

English   Western   Show Jumping   Endurance

Dressage   Polo   Natural Horsemanship

Types of Horses Used:

Marwari and Kathiawari horses (hot blooded)

FUEL
YOUR
SOUL
WITH
HORSE RIDING

www.wadirum—stable.com
+33 6 16 29 30 04

Jordan

Wadi Rum Ride

This 8 night's trip which includes 5 full riding days in Wadi Rum is our most popular ride. This ride covers most of the Wadi Rum Protected Area with a changing landscape all the time. Petra visit, and 3 hotels nights.

Riding level:
- Intermediate rider
- Camels on request for non riders
- Trekking on request for non riders

www.wadirum-stable.com
Rideinjordan@gmail.com

Wadi Rum Stable:

Oct-May

1-3 hours   3-5 hours   5+ hours   variety

Beginners   Experienced

Intermediate   Non-Riders
                Welcome

English   Western   Show Jumping   Endurance

Dressage   Polo   Natural
                        Horsemanship

Types of Horses Used:

Arabians

Mongolia

Read our Stories or Listen to the Audio Books about Riding in Mongolia and the Mongol Derby by Equestrian Adventuresses on:

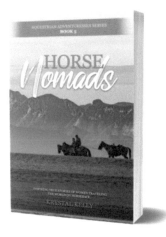

www.EquestrianAdventuresses.com

Stone Horse Expeditions

Riding Adventures in Mongolia! Morning breaks to the quiet sound of wranglers preparing our own handmade saddles and trusted horses for the day's ride. Breakfast is being made and guests rise to a new day of adventure.

We set off through fields of wildflowers, crossing rivers, over mountain passes, discovering something new with each horizon. Matching horses to a rider's ability and traveling at a varied pace as the terrain dictates. Walk, trot, gallop, there is opportunity for novice to expert on each ride.

The day ends with a glass of wine and a good meal.

https://stonehorsemongolia.com

Stone Horse Expeditions:

June - Oct

1-3 hours   3-5 hours   5+ hours   variety

Beginners   Experienced

Intermediate   Non-Riders Welcome

English   Western   Show Jumping   Endurance

Dressage   Polo   Natural Horsemanship

Types of Horses Used:

Mongolian horses, typically 14 hands, amazing endurance, easygoing characters, all seasoned trail horses.

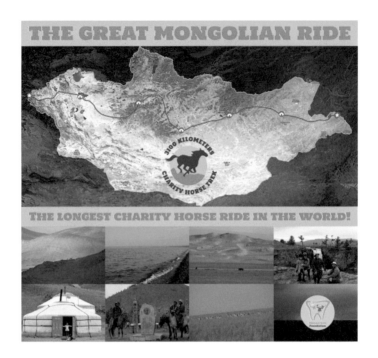

The Great Mongolian Ride

The longest charity horse ride in the world! And you can be a part... A charity horse ride from the far West of Mongolia in the Altai Mountains to the Eastern most tip of the country in the open grassy plains of Dornod. A total of 3100km, traversing the full width of Mongolia. Join for the whole 10 week expedition or for a short 10 day sprint. This is a one-time charity challenge, a once in a lifetime chance and completely unique experience, all for an amazing cause. Misheel Kids Foundation is the sole beneficiary of this Charity Ride, receiving 20% of proceeds. Misheel Kids Foundation provides much needed dental care for disadvantaged children in Mongolia. http://misheel-kids-foundation.com/de/ Our annual Mongolian horse treks are listed on our Website, the dates can be handled flexibly for 2021 and the trek will take place in 2022.

www.saraas-horse-trek-mongolia.com

The Great Mongolian Ride:

July to September

1-3 hours   3-5 hours   5+ hours   variety

Beginners

Experienced

Intermediate

Non-Riders
Welcome

English   Western   Show Jumping   Endurance

Dressage   Polo   Natural Horsemanship

Types of Horses Used:

Mongolian horses, typically 14 hands, similar to Icelandinc horses.

New Zealand

Kia Ora Adventure Horse Trekking

We are a boutique multiday horseback adventure company deep in the heart of the southern alps New Zealand. Kiwi to the core our company purpose breeds horses recreating the original "station bred" horses utilised by the pioneers who travelled to Aotearoa. With breath-taking locations from 2 to 11 day adventures take you far from the tourist routes to explore:

- High Mountain Peaks through the forgotten pack trails threaded through the mountain peaks
- Glacial lakes and rivers so clear you can see the trout playing beneath the waves
- Tussock filled hidden valleys flanked by imposing mountain ranges
- Transportation to/from trails (T & C's apply to suit the trail)
- Historic Accommodation that tells the stories of the trails
- Farm fresh foods that warm your soul at the end of the day in the saddle

Digital detox to refresh your mind as you are enveloped in Papatuanuku "Mother Earth" astounding beauty. Team up with our adventure horses, relax into the saddle and let your troubles blow away in the mountain air.

adventurehorsetrekkingnz@farmside.co.nz
www.adventurehorsetrekking.co.nz/

Kia Ora Adventure Horse Trekking:

Nov-May

1-3 hours   3-5 hours   5+ hours   variety

Beginners   Experienced

Intermediate   Non-Riders Welcome

English   Western   Show Jumping   Endurance

Dressage   Polo   Natural Horsemanship

Nicaragua

BIG SKY RANCH
N I C A R A G U A

Beach Rides
Mountain Rides
Full Moon Rides
Monkey Viewing Rides

discover Nicaragua
on horseback

www.bigskyranchnicaragua.com

www.bigskyranchnicaragua.com

Big Sky Ranch

Famed for its surf breaks, friendly locals and emerging eco-tourism - Nicaragua happens to also offer plenty of picture-perfect beaches ideal for horse riding year round. Big Sky Ranch invites you to Grab Life by the Reins and dare to explore.

Big Sky Ranch in southern Nicaragua is ideal for your Central American riding holiday. A popular choice for rides in this region combine riding at the beach, river rides for monkey viewing and the tropical forested hills with spectacular views along the coast. Nicaragua is considered Central America's up and coming destination and attracts all types of travelers – families included.

Left untouched, wild, and underdeveloped - the beach riding here is truly epic. Surfers use the beaches at high tide however riding is best at low tide meaning riders regularly have the entire beach to themselves. Horse adventures at Big Sky Ranch include Full Moon Rides with beach fire, Overnight Camping, Horse Surfing and Star Gazing rides.

Big Sky Ranch caters to both Western and English riding. Horses are mostly rescue horses that have grown strong and healthy and enjoy what they do.

Are you a confident canterer? Big Sky Ranch comes highly recommended if you're looking for a thoroughly satisfying experience cantering through the surf. Beginners need not worry though, there are paths along relaxing woodlands to explore and plenty of beaches in the area that cater to all levels. And there's no need to pack your boots. Big Sky Ranch has boots, jeans, helmets, and cowboy hats.

Big Sky Ranch is an equestrian community just 10km from the small surf town of San Juan del Sur. For those who wish to do multi-day riding, there are plenty of options in the area for accommodation with yoga, infinity pools, catering, surf lessons, fishing, sailing and countless adventures. Looking for a lifestyle change, check out options for owning.

http://www.bigskyranchnicaragua.com
ride@bigskyranchnicaragua.com

Big Sky Ranch:

    Avoid October
(Rainy Season)

 1-3 hours   3-5 hours   5+ hours   variety

Beginners

Experienced

 Intermediate

Non-Riders
Welcome

 English   Western   Show Jumping   Endurance

Dressage   Polo   Natural
Horsemanship

Oman

Happy Travels Oman

Explore the Sultanate of Oman on the horseback!

From the lively city of Muscat to the golden sand dunes of the South, Oman is a mesmerizing blend of old Arabia and the current world. A fabulous country to visit with mountain ranges, wadis, desert and the sea and, according to the legend home of Sinbad the Sailor. Oman has retained its ancient atmosphere and mystique; now is the time to visit! An exciting new ride in the Sultanate of Oman often referred to as "The Jewel of the Arabian Gulf".

It is a nice ride covering the north part of Wahiba sand. Our camp is moving every day; we are covering 25 KM per day and our local team preparing food and nice campfire for long evening!

The Wahiba, a huge desert of 10,000 square km. This is a real challenge for all but the perfect place to spend time with the Bedu who have inhabited this desert for centuries. The Omanis Bedus are very proud and hospitality is an important part of their way of life.

info@happytravelsoman.com
www.happytravelsoman.com

Happy Travels Oman:

Oct-March

1-3 hours   3-5 hours   5+ hours   variety

Beginners   Experienced

Intermediate   Non-Riders
                   Welcome

English   Western   Show Jumping   Endurance

Dressage   Polo   Natural
                            Horsemanship

Types of Horses Used:

Arabians

Peru

Hacienda del Chalán

Ride on smooth Paso Horses through the Peruvian Andes. From the Sacred Valley of the Incas, archeological complexes and Salt-flats riding to amazing viewpoints with snow-mountains and adventurous rock formations with condors. Meet local people and learn about ancient Inca culture while riding through beautiful and rough nature.

Tours: 2-6 days. Accommodation: hostels, local communities, tents. Good food!

www.haciendadelchalan.com
reservas@haciendadelchalan.com

Hacienda del Chalán:

April - Dec

1-3 hours   3-5 hours   5+ hours   variety

Beginners

Experienced

Intermediate

Non-Riders Welcome

English   Western   Show Jumping   Endurance

Dressage   Polo   Natural Horsemanship

Types of Horses Used:

Warm blood Peruvian Paso Horses. Our horses are gaited and you will be doing a lot of trotting (gaited) which is very comfortable to ride!

Romania

Read our Stories or Listen to the Audio Books about Riding in Romania by Equestrian Adventuresses on:

www.EquestrianAdventuresses.com

Ivó Riding Ranch

Horseback riding is an integral part of the traditional Transylvanian scene and the naturally gentle Icelandic horse provides excellent riding opportunities. We have chosen the Icelandic Horse because of its gentle, friendly disposition and calm manner that make them a delight for anyone to ride. Their two unique gaits, the tölt and the flying pace, provide a remarkably smooth way to travel over rugged terrain, making long hours in the saddle more comfortable. We organize trips in the surrounding mountains enyoing the mountain pour nature. Our riding tours are recommended for experimented riders. During our multiple day tours the bags and the luggage of the participants are transported by car to the accommodations. On the multiple day riding tours the prices include accommodation, food and non alcoholic beverages. Accomodation is in our house, Honor Villa (www.honorvilla.ro). Transfer from the main airports (Bucharest, Cluj, Sibiu, Tg. Mures, Bacau) are included in our offers. Our 35 iclandic horses (www.izlandilovak.ro) are waiting for you. Leave your stressful life behind and explore a hidden place away from the tourist rush and off the beaten path. For any information and booking send me an email to activity@elkfarm.ro or call me on +40 756094251.

www.izlandilovak.ro

Ivó Riding Ranch:

June-July,
Sept-Oct

1-3 hours   3-5 hours   5+ hours   variety

Beginners

Experienced

Intermediate

Non-Riders
Welcome

English   Western   Show Jumping   Endurance

Dressage   Polo   Natural
Horsemanship

Types of Horses Used:

Icelandic horses so expect lots of Tolt -- their smooth gait

Slovenia

Horses on Breg

Unspoiled nature, exciting adventures, horse riding. Does this sound like your dream holiday?

We know that wide-open skies and beautiful landscapes are best experienced from the saddle.

If you are a person with a love for the outdoors, a sense of adventure and a passion for horses, this is the right place for you. A holiday isn't a holiday without time spent on a horseback.

Our scenic riding programmes are an absolute dream for those who love nature and beautiful landscapes – the Karst region is incredibly green with varied terrain, hidden treasures and spectacular wildlife.

horsesonbreg.si

Horses on Breg:

March - Oct

1-3 hours   3-5 hours   5+ hours   variety

Beginners   Experienced

Intermediate   Non-Riders Welcome

English   Western   Show Jumping   Endurance

Dressage   Polo   Natural Horsemanship

Types of Horses Used:

Warmblood, Quarerhorses, and Icelandic horses

Spain

www.imagineriding.com

Imagine Riding

An unusual opportunity: this ride in western Spain was created for Imagine Riding by a professional forester, guide and wildlife manager ('Ingeniero de Montes') who was raised in Extremadura.

Intimately acquainted with the landscape and trails of northern and western Spain it will be his pleasure to share his knowledge and expertise with us on the trail.

We will ride Lusitano, Arabian and PRE trekking horses bred in these mountains and trained by a Gredos horseman whose father still led his cattle along the Transhumance route each spring and autumn.

We will follow in the path of the great Hapsburg Emperor Charles V, who in 1556 AD retired to the Monastery of Yuste. The route takes us through the Gredos range. We travel along Roman roads, cattle ways, mountain trails and alpine plains, crossing stone bridges and passing villages along the way. Overnights are in historic manor houses and 'parador' castles. A mid-mountain ride with opportunities for faster riding each day.

September 26 - October 03, 2021
Refundable deposits or change to a later date if the ride is impacted by Covid-19.

www.imagineriding.com
imagineriding1@gmail.com

Imagine Horse Riding:

April - July,
Sept - Nov

1-3 hours   3-5 hours   5+ hours   variety

Beginners   Experienced

Intermediate   Non-Riders
Welcome

English   Western   Show Jumping   Endurance

Dressage   Polo   Natural
Horsemanship

Types of Horses Used:

PRE . Lusitano and crossbreeds

Turkey

www.imagineriding.com

Imagine Riding

Did you ever wonder where the mythical King Midas may have hidden his gold?

If you travel to NW Anatolia in Turkey, you will discover ancient Phrygia, once the most powerful kingdom of the Near East.

It is here that King Midas is said to have reigned during its golden age.

You can read about this in the works of Homer and Herodotus or better yet, you can come see for yourself as you ride

along the ancient tracks that crisscross this valley. We travel through ever-changing scenery. Rock hewn temples and ancient burial tombs are scattered throughout. Strange volcanic rock formations and fairy chimneys line our path. Ever onwards we ride alongside riverbanks, lakes and on forests ways once crossed by the caravans, kings and armies of ancient times. Turkish Arabian and Arabian cross endurance horses, fit and forward-going are our reliable steeds.

This one of kind ten-day journey has only been done twice before on horseback. It is a camping expedition with a backup team looking after all of our needs
 as we follow these historic and eerily beautiful paths. It is an adventure of a lifetime.

We are planning this ride going in both directions: May 07-16 and May 21- 30, 2022

www.imagineriding.com
imagineriding1@gmail.com

Imagine Horse Riding:

April - July,
Sept - Nov

1-3 hours   3-5 hours   5+ hours   variety

Beginners   Experienced

Intermediate   Non-Riders
Welcome

English   Western   Show Jumping   Endurance

Dressage   Polo   Natural
Horsemanship

Types of Horses Used:

Arabian and Arabian Crosses

U.S.A

California

San Diego Horse Trail Riding

WE OFFER PRIVATE GUIDED TOURS VIA HORSEBACK. WE MOSTLY RIDE THROUGH THE CLEVELAND NATIONAL FOREST IN SOUTHERN CALIFORNIA.

For bookings visit my website: www.sandiegohorsetrailriding.com

San Diego Horse Trail Riding:

All Year Round

1-3 hours   3-5 hours   5+ hours   variety

Beginners   Experienced

Intermediate   Non-Riders Welcome

English   Western   Show Jumping   Endurance

Dressage   Polo   Natural Horsemanship

Types of Horses Used:

We customize each private guided trail ride to the customers' riding experience.

Missouri

www.brushycreeklodge.com

Brushy Creek

Here at Brushy Creek Lodge we offer a true western experience with southern hospitality. You'll delight in the freedom to do a little bit of everything or nothing at all. Our facilities are available year round for your convenience. We have over 130 miles of trails for you and your horses to explore! Our property backs up to the Mark Twain National Forest and all of our trails are linked to the Ozark Trail! Whether you're a first-timer in these parts or a native there are plenty of exciting and beautiful places to explore. If you can drag yourself away from our camping, trail rides, nature hikes, and swimming, then just ask one of our staff and they will point you in the right direction. You'll want to see the majestic Johnson Shut-Ins State Park, Sam A Baker Park, Elephant Rocks, Taum Sauk State Park, go floating at Parks Bluff Campground, or visit any one of the several beautiful locations that our area has to offer! All within minutes of Brushy Creek.

www.brushycreeklodge.com
info@vsfoxtrot.com

Brushy Creek:

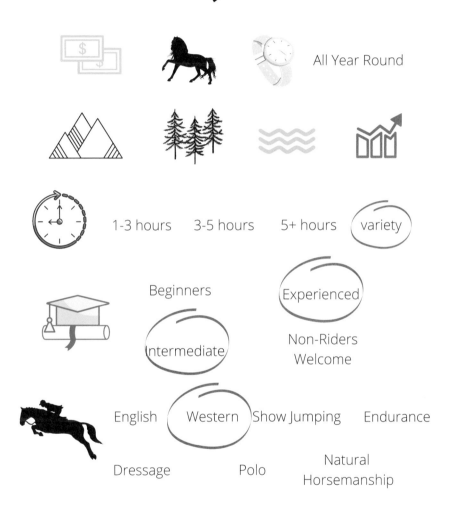

All Year Round

1-3 hours   3-5 hours   5+ hours   variety

Beginners   Experienced

Intermediate

Non-Riders
Welcome

English   Western   Show Jumping   Endurance

Dressage   Polo   Natural
Horsemanship

Types of Horses Used:

Fox Trotters

Travel Agents

www.africanhorsesafaris.com

African Horse Safaris

Do you dream of galloping over endless savannahs with herds of zebra and giraffe? Have you imagined yourself riding alongside the giant tusker elephants in East Africa or splashy canters through the flood waters of the Okavango Delta? Do you want to ride across vast landscapes with no sign of human life besides the grinning faces of the riders alongside you?

African Horse Safaris offers the largest portfolio of expertly guided and unique horse experiences across the African continent. With us, you'll discover Africa's most iconic horse-riding holidays - and a few best kept secrets. We warn you, Africa is highly addictive and exploring it on horseback is an unforgettable experience!

Our handpicked rides combine unrivalled adventure, professional guiding, quality accommodation and horses that are as important as the guests. We have personally tried and tested all our safaris, so we can give you great comparisons and first-hand advice. If you have been riding since you could walk, or are new to the sport, we have a horse-riding holiday to suit you! Whether you are travelling solo, with a group of friends, your family or even with non-riding partner, our safari-gurus can guide you to the perfect adventure.

Africa is a kaleidoscope of different landscapes just waiting to be explored and there is no better way than exploring it on horseback. Whether it's galloping across the endless Namib desert with your heartbeat matching your horses' thundering hooves or feeling your heart stop as you stand watching a pride of lions on the plains of Kenya - There is no greater freedom than exploring Africa on horseback!

Join us - Your adventure awaits!

Website: www.africanhorsesafaris.com
Email: isabel@africanhorsesafaris.com
Instagram: @africanhorsesafaris

African Horse Safaris

11 Countries – Endless Adventures

Botswana –Ride through Africa's Eden with exciting wildlife and unique landscapes

Eswatini – Mountainous adventure through Africa's last forgotten kingdoms

Egypt – Authentic journey through The Land of the Pharaohs on fiery Arabs

Kenya – Embark on a horseback expedition filled with Lion King moments

Morocco – Endless deserts, ancient history and thrilling riding on Arab Stallions

Mozambique – Laid back riding and horseback swims in tropical paradise

Namibia – Mind-blowing landscapes, desert adapted wildlife and eye-watering gallops

South Africa – Sensational riding through varied landscapes

Tanzania – Wide open plains and exciting wildlife encounters

Uganda – Discover wild jungles, rural villages and the source of the River Nile

Zimbabwe – Tumbling waterfalls, unique culture and riding with incredible wildlife

www.africanhorsesafaris.com
isabel@africanhorsesafaris.com

African Horse Safaris:

All Year Round

1-3 hours   3-5 hours   5+ hours   variety

Beginners   Experienced

Intermediate   Non-Riders Welcome

English   Western   Show Jumping   Endurance

Dressage   Polo   Natural Horsemanship

Accommodation: Tented Camps / Lodges / Guesthouses. Ride Type: Progressive / Lodge Based

www.imagineriding.com

Imagine Horse Riding

Life is an adventure. And horse-riding on known or yet to be discovered ground is the best adventure in life.

Our mission is to seek out the finest rides. We search for authenticity and connection. Connection with the people we meet, the horses we ride, the landscapes we cross.

We are strong on passion, intuition and imagination, and always open to new adventures.
We are a nimble and curious and like nothing more than curating and crafting new experiences or making existing rides even more enjoyable.
We constantly explore new paths with our outfitters and fashion them into new trails.

There are a number of ways to experience journeys on horseback and cultures rich in equine traditions. Each has its own beauty — it all depends on your preferences.

On our camping expeditions, beyond the beautiful vistas it might well be the multiple sensations of being in nature, with each other, and with the horses that leave the most lasting memories.

Our trail rides offer similar adventure, but you get to sleep in a comfortable bed. You get a hot shower each day. And you get to dress for dinner. Sometimes though we'll throw in a night or two of glamping – just enough to get a taste of it but not enough to hate it.

On our centre-based rides we stay mostly at the horse centre or farm and ride in a different direction each day. Plenty of time is left to take in cultural and historical sites, enjoy in a local festival, meander through an old town after a day in the saddle or hang out with the locals over a glass of wine.

www.imagineriding.com
@imagine_riding

Imagine Horse Riding

We nurture a close connection with the outfitters that we have come to know over time and spend a lot of time sourcing those rare 'truffles'

No matter how you choose to travel on horseback, we look for what is authentic and true, seeking out the hidden, the simple and the surprising.

Susan Wirth, the founder of Imagine Riding has a vast trove of experience having ridden all over the world and completed and organized many long-distance rides herself. She developed a deep passion for this mode of travel and its many rewards. It invites slowness. It encourages focus. It grounds you. And it gives you access to places and moments that most people may never know.

Contact:
Susan Wirth
imagineriding1@gmail.com
+917-399-8184
www.imagineriding.com
@imagine_riding

Imagine Horse Riding:

All Year Round

1-3 hours   3-5 hours   5+ hours   variety

Beginners

Experienced

Intermediate

Non-Riders Welcome

English   Western   Show Jumping   Endurance

Dressage   Polo   Natural Horsemanship

Every Country in the World Index A-Z

A

Afghanistan

- silkroadafghanistan.com

Albania

- http://bit.ly/horse-tours
  horseridingalbania.com

Andorra

- www.hipica-aldosa.com/en/
  content/riding-holidays-heart-
  pyrenees
- en.hotansa.com
- equi-libre.fr/site/

Antigua and Barbuda

www.antiguaequestrian.com

Argentina

- http://bit.ly/horse-tours
- www.horseridingtierradelfuego
  .com
- www.latardepolo.com
- ampascachi.com
- argentinapoloday.com.ar/en/
  polo-club

- www.estanciadonjoaquin.com.
  ar
- www.paloaltopolo.com
- www.theargentinaspecialists.co
  m/what-to-do/horse-riding
- www.estanciaalinco.com

Armenia

- http://bit.ly/horse-tours

Australia

- http://bit.ly/horse-tours
  www.centennialglenstables.co
  m
- www.cowboyup.com.au
- www.hepburnlagoonrides.com.
  au
  bogonghorsebackadventures.w
  eebly.com
- cradleadventures.com.au
- diggersreststation.com.au/
  horse-riding-holidays/
- www.horsetreks.com.au
- www.rbhr.com.au
- www.thredbovalleyhorseriding.
  com
- buckleupbushrides.com.au/
- facebook.com/eqwineescapes/

Austria

- www.edelweiss-gurgl.com/en/
  hotel/riding-stables

- www.pferdehof-koaserminerl.at/horseback_riding.html
- www.sno.co.uk/lakes-mountains-holidays/austria/best-horse-riding/
- www.wiesenhof.at/en/lake-achensee/horse-riding-austria/61-0.html

Azerbaijan

- www.caucasus-expedition.com/en/

B

Bahamas

- pinetree-stables.com
- www.ridingbahamas.com

Bahrain

- dilmun-club.com
- twinpalmsridingcentre.com
- www.facebook.com/Awali-Riding-Club-164023736963838/
- www.shakhooraridingcentre.com

Barbados

- www.barbadoshorseriding.com
- www.facebook.com/pages/category/Horse-Riding-School/Sandy-Turf-Stables-Barbados-100856654013319/

Belarus

- koni.yadro.by
- mustang-club.by
- agrohutor.jimdo.com

Belgium

- http://bit.ly/horse-tours
  www.franciscushof.be
- www.horsetrailriding.be
- www.ranch.be/pages/nl/de-ranch.php

Belize

- http://bit.ly/horse-tours
- metbelize.com
- www.hannastables.com/horseback-rides/
- www.outbacktrails.com
- www.bananabank.com

Bhutan

- www.windhorsetours.com

Bolivia

- tupizatours.com
- www.facebook.com/horsebackridingsucre/

Bosnia and Herzegovina

- http://bit.ly/horse-tours
- www.jahanje.ba
- kkhidalgo.com/en/horseback-riding-lessons-sarajevo/

- www.lazyhorse.ba/en/index.html

Botswana

- www.africanhorseback.com
- www.ridebotswana.com
- www.okavangodelta.com/tours-safaris/african-horseback-safaris/

Brazil

- http://bit.ly/horse-tours
- www.ridingbrazil.com
- www.harasype.com/

Brunei

- www.bruneibay.net/the_royal_experience/equestrianpark.html
- www.facebook.com/Beq-Equestrian-Centre-Sdn-Bhd-246722882021360/

Bulgaria

- http://bit.ly/horse-tours
  horseridingbulgaria.com
- www.horse-riding-bg.com/home/
- sakarhorsefarm.com/

Burkina Faso

- www.chevalmandingue.com
- fasoducheval.wordpress.com
- www.facebook.com/clubdeletrier

C

Cabo Verde

- www.horseexcursionsal.com

Cambodia

- www.thehappyranch.com

Cameroon

- www.facebook.com/clubsaintgeorges/

Canada

- http://bit.ly/horse-tours
  9fingerranch.com
- boundaryranch.com
- trailridevacations.com
- www.vancouverhorsebackriding.com
- horseback.com
- www.alpinestables.com
- www.brokenrailranch.com/contacthours.html
- www.facebook.com/groups/FireAndIceTours
- www.flyingu.com
- www.horseplayniagara.com

Chile

- http://bit.ly/horse-tours
  estanciaspatagonia.com
- www.andesridingchile.com
- www.chile-horseriding.com
- horseridingchile.com
- www.cabalgatasantiago.com
- www.campesano.com

- www.chileofftrack.com/contact-us/
- www.ecuestresanpedro.cl
- www.estanciaspatagonia.com

China

- www.equriding.com
- www.goldinmetropolitanhotel.com/hotel/index.php
- www.langmusi.net
- www.tibetanbarley.com/horsetrekking

Colombia

- http://bit.ly/horse-tours
- www.facebook.com/lajuanacolombia/cabalgatassanpablosalento.com
- horseshoe-colombia.com
- ridingcolombia.com/en
- www.aventurecotours.com
- www.cabalgataselcarmelo.com
- www.valleverdehorseriding.com

Costa Rica

- http://bit.ly/horse-tours establosanrafael.com
- haciendamilbellezas.com
- www.caribehorse.com
- www.horseback-riding-tour.com
- www.paintedponyguestranch.com
- www.playachiquitaridingadventures.com
- www.theridingadventure.com
- www.tokpelacostarica.com
- barkinghorsefarm.com
- centauracr.com
- ranchotropical.com

- www.costaricaequestrianvacation.com
- www.crbeachbarn.com
- www.fincacaballoloco.com
- www.horsejungle.com
- www.horseridecostarica.com
- www.horsetrekmonteverde.com

Cote D'Ivoire

- www.facebook.com/Club-Saint-Michel-197339486949755/
- www.facebook.com/poneyclubgolf

Croatia

- http://bit.ly/horse-tours
- istrastar.com/hr/Default.aspx
- kojankoral.com/en/
- ranch-chivas.com
- www.equestrianclubsplit.com
- liska-adventure-riding.business.site
- www.horseridingzadar.com
- www.lindenretreat.com/activities/horse-riding-croatia/

Cuba

- www.facebook.com/RanchoElDajao
- horseridinginvinales.com/en/

Cyprus

- www.horseridingpaphos.com
- www.paphosec.com
- georgesranchcyprus.com
- www.aphroditehillsridingclub.com/default.html

Czech Republic

- www.jk-slupenec.cz/1/en/normal/home/
- www.konevondrov.cz
- favory.cz
- www.giant-mountains.info/sport/horse-riding.html
- www.konerasna.cz/en/contact/
- www.ludvikovcz.com
- www.hospodarskydvur.cz

D

Democratic Republic of the Congo

- chk-kinshasa.com

Denmark

- http://bit.ly/horse-tours
- copenhagen-horsebackriding.com/
- cphpolo.com/polo-course/
- sagaheste.com/
- www.riding-greenland.com

Dominica

- brandymanor.wixsite.com/riding-center
- www.rainforestriding.com

Dominican Republic

- www.rancholorilar1.com/

- rudysrancho.com/
- www.horseplaypuntacana.com

E

Ecuador

- greenhorseranch.zohosites.com
- www.rideandes.com
- www.centroecuestrebellavista.com/

Egypt

- http://bit.ly/horse-tours www.equestriandreamegypt.com/en/
- www.facebook.com/egypthorseridingphoto/
- www.horsesandhieroglyphs.com
- www.wolkes-horse-paradise-hurghada.de/

Estonia

- http://bit.ly/horse-tours
- www.kuusekannuratsatalu.ee/index.php?lang=en

Eswatini

- biggameparks.org
- www.nyanza.co.sz
- www.africanhorsesafaris.com

Ethiopia

- www.bekaferdaranch.com/

F

Fiji

- www.facebook.com/coralcoasthorseridingadventurcoralcoasthorseriding/

Finland

- http://bit.ly/horse-tours www.ridenorth.fi/short.html
- www.yllaksenvaellushevoset.fi
- www.lapinsaaga.fi

France

- http://bit.ly/horse-tours
- fonluc.com/
- tourainecheval.com/index.html
- www.horseinthecity.fr/en/homepage.html
- www.domaine-equestre-des-bastides.fr/index.php/fr
- www.frenchridingholidays.co.uk

G

Gambia

- kotuhorses.mozello.com/contact/

Georgia

- www.lostridgeinn.com/tours/

- www.facebook.com/horseparadisegeorgia/
- facebook.com/horseridingtbilisi
- www.facebook.com/Jalabauri/
- www.wyprawygruzja.pl/

Germany

- http://bit.ly/horse-tours
- reiterferien-bayern.eu
- www.goedelsteinhof.de
- www.oldriverranch.de
- www.lucky-trails.de
- www.stone-hill-ranch.de
- www.triple-mountain-ranch.de

Ghana

- www.greenranchlakebosomtwe.com/contactus

Greece

- http://bit.ly/horse-tours
- www.horseridingparos.com
- www.ipposmolyvos.com
- www.trailriderscorfu.com
- www.erikashorsefarm.gr
- www.hersonissos-horseriding.com/
- www.horseriding.gr
- www.poseidonion.com/en/horse-riding
- toumba.gr/
- mykonoshorse.com/

Greenland

- www.riding-greenland.com

Guatemala

- ravenscroftstables.wixsite.com
- www.facebook.com/pg/AtFincaXetuc/about/?ref=page_internal
- www.unicornioazul.com/

H

Honduras

- beachclubroatan.com/
- redridgestable.com

Hong Kong

- www.hkhorseriding.com

Hungary

- trailriding.hu
- www.koronatours.hu/english
- lazarlovaspark.hu/en/

I

Iceland

- http://bit.ly/horse-tours
- hestaland.net
- islenskihesturinn.is/

India

- http://bit.ly/horse-tours
- mandawasafaris.in
- revantamarwarihorses.com
- www.krossterrain.com
- www.princesstrails.com
- japalouppe.com
- www.horseindia.com
- www.krishnaranch.com
- www.roopniwaskothi.com/
- www.naturalhorsemanshipindia.com
- www.kutchclassicridercamp.com

Indonesia

- http://bit.ly/horse-tours www.baliequestriancentre.com
- www.kudapstables.com/
- www.truebaliexperience.com/
- horseridinginbali.com
- www.ubudhorsestables.com/index.html
- www.facebook.com/gilimenohorseriding/
- saltycowboy.org/

Iran

- triptopersia.com/iran-tours/iran-horse-riding-tours
- www.uppersia.com/

Iraq

- erbilhorseclub.com

Ireland

- http://bit.ly/horse-tours
- coopershilllivery.wixsite.com
- irishhorseriding.com
- www.irelandonhorseback.com
- www.kilkeacastle.ie

- www.leevalleyequestriancentre.ie
- horse-holiday-farm.com
- www.ashfordcastle.com
- www.clareequestrian.com
- www.killarneyridingstables.com
- www.sheanshorsefarm.com/

Israel

- www.horseride.co.il/horseback-riding-israel/
- www.ride-israel.com

Italy

- http://bit.ly/horse-tours www.cornacchino.it/en/start.html
- horseback.it/index.html
- www.facebook.com/ilgelsominoranch/
- toscanatrail.de/en/home-uk/
- www.ridesicily.eu/en
- chiantiriding.it/
- www.tharerwirt.com/en

J

Jamaica

- www.halfmoon.com
- www.hooves-jamaica.com/
- www.reggaehorsebackriding.com/

Japan

- horsetrekking.jp/

- ie-horse.wixsite.com/ieuma/english
- www.jphorseriding.com/

Jordan

- www.jordan-horseridingholidays.com/
- horseridingtoursjordan.com/
- jordantracks.com
- www.jordan-desert-journeys.com
- www.jordanartisttours.com
- www.terhaal.com/contact-us

K

Kazakhstan

astanatours.kz/
www.poloclub.kz/

Kenya

- www.offbeatsafaris.com
- safarisunlimited.com
- www.ridinghighkenya.com

Kuwait

- horsebackridingkuwait.com
- www.facebook.com/kuwaitrc/

Kyrgyzstan

- karakolhorsetrekking.blogspot.com/
- kyrgyzriders.com/
- www.kyrgyztrek.com

- www.facebook.com/
  kyrgyzwonders/

L

Latvia

- www.adventureride.eu/en/
  home
- www.darzini.lv/index.php

Lebanon

- lebaneseequestriancenter.com
- www.chl-lebanon.com/6.html
- www.equestrian-circle.com
- www.facebook.com/
  CedarsHorseRiding/

Lesotho

- www.drakensberg.org/listing/
  dragons-landing/
- malealea.com
- www.underberghorsetrailsands
  afaris.com
- www.facebook.com/
  wulkifarms/

Liechtenstein

- www.liechtensteinpolo.com/
  polo-club

Lithuania

- pakruojo-dvaras.lt/en/stud

Luxembourg

- www.mullerthal.lu/en

M

Madagascar

- www.chevalnosybe.com
- www.facebook.com/
  fakaranchfedrova/
- www.facebook.com/
  fanirinaranch/

Malawi

- www.plateaustables.com/
  Rates.html

Malaysia

- www.langkawihorses.com/

Malta

- www.goldenbayhorseriding.co
  m/
- www.linostables.com/
- gozostables.com/

Mauritius

- www.harasdumorne.com/
- www.maritimresortandspa.mu
  /en/activities-leisure/
  equestrian-centre/overview
- www.centreequestrederiambel.
  com/

Mexico

- http://bit.ly/horse-tours
- www.horsebackmexico.com/contact-us
- www.ranchocarisuva.com/
- rancholascascadas.com

Moldova

- sparta-club.md
- www.facebook.com/kskbalti/
- www.travel-chisinau.com/activities/horseback-riding.html

Mongolia

- http://bit.ly/horse-tours
- www.horsetrekmongolia.com
- www.zavkhan.co.uk
- stonehorsemongolia.com
- saraas-horse-trek-mongolia.com
- www.adastraadventures.com
- www.gobidesertcup.com

Montenegro

- http://bit.ly/horse-tours
- www.mountainriders.me

Morocco

- http://bit.ly/horse-tours
- amodoucheval.com/
- les2gazelles.com/en/
- www.zouina-cheval.com
- www.equievasion.com
- www.marocacheval.com

Mozambique

- www.mozambiquehorsesafari.com
- www.tofoinfo.com/horse-riding

Myanmar

- www.ayeindamartour.com
- bagandaytours.com/bagan-adventure-tours/bagan-horse-riding-tours/
- www.inlehorseclub.com

N

Namibia

- www.okakambe.iway.na/
- gross-okandjou.de/
- www.kuzikus-namibia.de/xe_activities_riding.html
- www.okapuka.com
- www.equitrails.org

Nepal

- http://bit.ly/horse-tours
- www.gokarna.com/horse-ride

Netherlands

- http://bit.ly/horse-tours
- www.de-boschhoeve.nl
- www.manegedemolenberg.nl
- www.nrsv.nl
- www.knhs.nl/sportaanbieders
- www.rijstaldeblinkert.nl/rijstal-de-blinkert/

- www.puur-terschelling.nl

New Zealand

- http://bit.ly/horse-tours adventurehorsetrekking.co.nz
- www.hanmerhorsetrekking.com
- thecardrona.co.nz
- www.facebook.com/ ngatunabackpackers/
- www.highcountryhorses.nz
- www.treklakeokareka.co.nz
- blueduckstation.co.nz/ activities/#horse-trekking

Nicaragua

- www.harishorsesnicaragua.com
- www.ranchochilamate.com

Niger

- clubequestredeniamey.blogspot.com

Nigeria

- lagospolo.com

North Macedonia

- http://bit.ly/horse-tours
- www.horseriding.com.mk

Norway

- http://bit.ly/horse-tours
- www.gullverkstallen.no/

- hovgard.no/en/
- www.mesna.no

O

Oman

- http://bit.ly/horse-tours
- www.oman-horseridingholidays.com

P

Pakistan

- m.facebook.com/ orrickhorseriding

Panama

- http://bit.ly/horse-tours www.bluffbeachretreat.com/ horseback-riding-in-bocas-del-toro/
- www.facebook.com/ junglecatpanama

Papua New Guinea

- www.papuanewguinea.travel/ koitaki-country-club

Paraguay

- cabana-austria.com/en/activities/

Peru

- http://bit.ly/horse-tours
  www.cuscoforyou.com
- www.haciendadelchalan.com
- www.horsebackridingcusco.com

Phillipines

- elkabayostables.com
- hhfequestrian.com/
- www.myboracayguide.com/boracay-activities/horse-riding/

Poland

- http://bit.ly/horse-tours
- www.sudety-trail.eu/horsetrails/

Portugal

- http://bit.ly/horse-tours
  rideandescape.com
- www.quintadasaudade.com
- lusitanotrailrides.jimdo.com
- www.montevelho.pt
- quintadofijo.eu/
- www.portugal-horse-riding.com/

Q

Qatar

- www.alshaqab.com

R

Republic of Korea

- skyranch.co.kr/kr/
- www.jejuhorse.com
- packagekorea.com/tour/horse-riding-tour/

Romania

- http://bit.ly/horse-tours
  english.husarslanic.com/
- nedeea-valceana.ro/
- www.cross-country.ro
- echitatiespiritulcailor.wordpress.com/
- lovasturakcsikorszagban.com/
- www.izlandilovak.ro

Russia

- http://bit.ly/horse-tours

Rwanda

- www.sengha.com/

S

San Marino

- centroequestrevalgiurata.blogspot.com

Saudi Arabia

- www.dirabgolf.com
- www.frusiya.com/
- www.lochnessriding.co.uk

Scotland, UK

- http://bit.ly/horse-tours
  www.wilderways.scot
- www.highlandsunbridled.com

Senegal

- www.espritdafrique-senegal.com

Serbia

- http://kentaur.club/en/
- www.konjickiklubarandjelovac.rs/sr-yu/

Seychelles

- www.turquoisehorsetrails.com

Singapore

- www.btsc.org.sg
- www.singaporepoloclub.org/

Slovakia

- www.skradne.sk

Slovenia

- http://bit.ly/horse-tours
- www.horsesonbreg.si
- en.pristava-lepena.com/horseback-riding
- www.ranc-mrcina.com/
- www.sloveniahorseriding.com/
- konji-na-bregu.business.site
- www.facebook.com/kmetijakolenc/
- www.lipica.org/en/

South Africa

- http://bit.ly/horse-tours
- horseridesatpetes.co.za
- www.facebook.com/TheHorseSafariCompany/
- www.blackhorsetrails.co.za/
- www.wildcoasthorsebackadventures.com
- africandreamhorsesafari.co.za
- heavenandearthtrails.co.za
- www.horseridingatpinkgeranium.com
- www.khotso.co.za
- www.moolmanshoek.co.za
- www.horseabout.co.za
- www.horsebackafrica.com
- www.ridejozi.co.za/
- www.ridinginafrica.com

Spain

- http://bit.ly/horse-tours
  haciendalaalegria.com/web/
- los-olivillos.com

- www.eponaspain.com/train-trail-horseback-riding/programme
- www.ridingholidaysspain.com
- bacchustravel.co.uk
- horseriding-holidays-andalucia.com/
- losalamosriding.co.uk
- naturacavall.com
- www.lareservaclubsotogrande.com/sotogrande/
- www.panorama-trails.com/en/
- www.proatur.com
- www.rideandalucia.net
- www.spain-horse-riding.com
- www.ecoslowexperience.com/trails
- www.ranchobonanza.es/
- caminosantiagoacaballo.com/en/

Sri Lanka

- forestpark.lk
- www.ceylonridingclub.com

St. Kitts & Nevis

- www.nevishorseback.com

St. Lucia

- holidayridingstablesstlucia.weebly.com
- www.atlanticridingstables.com
- www.eastcoaststable.com

St. Vincent & Grenadines

- www.mustique-island.com/activities/equestrian/

Suriname

- www.facebook.com/clubneutraal/
- www.facebook.com/Rimboe-horse-World-Suriname-353037708201515/

Sweden

- http://bit.ly/horse-tours
- www.horsesoftaiga.com
- www.ourlittlefarm.se

Switzerland

- chevaux-gruyeres.ch/
- www.engadin-riverranch.ch/index.php/de/
- www.leventinawestern.ch/
- www.engadin-reiten.ch

T

Tajikistan

- www.pamirhorseadventure.com/horse-riding-2/

Thailand

- www.phukethorseclub.com/
- www.phuketridingclub.com/
- www.webjipata.tht.me/
- www.daytripchiangmai.com
- www.southarabianhorseclub.com/
- www.facebook.com/ChaowanatHorseFarm/

Trinidad and Tobago

- www.being-with-horses.com/
- www.facebook.com/ SaddleValleyStables/
- www.friendshipridingstables.com

Tunisia

- mezrayaranch.com
- ranchyassmina.wixsite.com/ home
- www.ranch-tanit-djerba.com/? lang=en
- djerbazitouna.com

Turkey

- http://bit.ly/horse-tours www.cappadociahorseriding.com/
- www.cemalranch.com/
- www.horseridingcappadocia.com
- akhal-tekehorsecenter.com
- www.moonlighthorseranch.com/

Turkmenistan

- ayan-travel.com

Turks & Caicos

- www.provoponies.com

U

United Arab Emirates

- www.dhabianequi.com
- www.aljiyadstables.com/
- www.stetson.com.ua/
- www.winnersequestrian.com/
- ddhre.webs.com/

Uganda

- nilehorsebacksafaris.com
- greengo-equestrian-club.business.site

Ukraine

- http://bit.ly/horse-tours
- horseback.kiev.ua/en
- idyllium.wixsite.com/alba

United Kingdom

- http://bit.ly/horse-tours www.adventureclydesdale.com
- www.blackhorses.co.uk
- www.cumbrianheavyhorses.com
- www.peerscloughpackhorses.co.uk
- www.tallyhostables.co.uk/
- www.transwales.com
- liberty-trails.com
- www.freerein.co.uk
- www.yourhorseadventures.co.uk
- www.wilderways.scot
- www.highlandsunbridled.com
- noltonstables.com

- www.islandriding.com/riding-holidays/
- ullswatersaddlebackhorsetrails.co.uk/

United Republic of Tanzania

- www.zanzibarhorseclub.com/
- www.facebook.com/MaishaMazuriHorseRidingClub
- www.facebook.com/MatambaFarm/
- www.kaskazihorsesafaris.com

Uruguay

- www.facebook.com/Cabalgatas-Villa-Serrana-434944423315189/

V

Vanuatu

- club-hippique-horse-riding.squarespace.com/
- www.bellevueranchvanuatu.com/
- www.facebook.com/pg/SantoHorseAdventures/about/

Venezuela

- www.cabatucan.com/
- www.haciendamacanao.com/

Vietnam

- nguahanoi.vn

W

Wales, UK

- noltonstables.com

Z

Zambia

- chundukwariverlodge.com/ride-zambezi/
- simalahahorsesafaris.com/

Zimbabwe

- volunteerencounter.com
- www.zambezihorsetrails.com
- www.lionandcheetahpark.com/stables
- ridezimbabwe.com

Every State in the USA Index A-Z

A

Alabama

- www.heartofdixietrailride.com
- www.southernhorsecarriages.com
- therustedroofbarn.com
- www.chooseyourgaitbreeding.com
- www.oakhollowfarm.net
- pairodocsfarm.com
- starlightstables.weebly.com
- twitter.comRiversideRanch3?
- starhbfarms.com

Alaska

- alaskahorseadventures.com
- sewardhorses.com
- www.alaskahorsemen.com
- www.denalihorsebacktours.com
- www.alaskantrailrides.com
- web.facebook.com/Trails-End-Horse-Adventures-136411483043630?_rdc=1&_rdr
- sunderlandranch.com
- cowgirlin75.wixsite.com
- akwalkers.com
- alaskahorseranch.com

Arizona

- http://bit.ly/horse-tours
  www.cavecreektrailrides.com
- trailhorseadventures.com
- www.arizona-horses.com
- arizonahorsebackadventures.com
- sedonahorsebackrides.com
- www.highmountaintrailrides.com
- www.tucsonhorsebackriding.com
- www.okcorrals.com
- www.cavecreekoutfitters.com
- www.saguarolakeranchstable.com
- www.boydranch.org/boyd-ranch-mule-ride/
- www.haciendadelsol.com

Arkansas

- www.hotsprings.org/places/arkansas-riding-stables
- www.horserentals.com
- www.flyingqfarms.com
- www.oktradingpost.com
- horsebackrideseurekaspringsar.com
- mountainharborridingstable.com
- www.sunshineacresranch.com
- holenthewallranch.com
- idlenook.com
- www.caneymountain.com

C

California

- horsenaroundtrailrides.com
- www.losangeleshorsebackriding.com
- www.sunshineanddaydream.com
- www.ridenorco.com
- www.jameszoppe.com
- redwoodhorserides.com
- westerntrailrides.org
- sandiegohorsetrailriding.com
- www.cctrailrides.com
- crescenttrailrides.com

Colorado

- http://bit.ly/horse-tours
  www.skhorses.com
- www.academyridingstables.com
- www.aastables.com
- tripleg.net
- www.highcountry-trails.com
- www.bearcreekstablescolorado.com
- www.rustyspurr.com
- ride.actionadventures.net
- www.bearmtnstables.com
- estesparkoutfitters.com
- elkheartoutfitters.com
- www.zranch.org
- www.cherokeeparkranch.com

Connecticut

- goldrushfarmsct.com
- bluesprucehorseriding.com
- www.windfieldmorganfarm.com
- www.valleyviewridingstables.com
- www.laurelledgefarm.com
- www.dreamcatcherfarmct.com
- www.grandviewfarms-ct.com
- www.meadfarm.com
- www.silverhorseshoestablesinc.com
- stirrupfunstables.com
- web.facebook.com/pgLucky-Chance-Farm-291203103147/about?ref=page_internal

D

Delaware

- cozyquartersfarm.com
- www.sunsetstable.com
- web.facebook.com/pages/Twin-Pines-Farm/162923903735548?_rdc=1&_rdr

F

Florida

- www.floridahorsebacktrailrides.com
- floridahorseriding.com
- aaadventurehorsetrails.com
- lazyhranch.net
- americanhorsetrails.us
- www.ocalatrailrides.com
- www.myakkatrailrides.com
- iiventuresevents.wixsite.com
- choycellc.com
- cponies.com
- www.hiddenpalmsranch.com
- www.orangeblossomtrailrides.com
- tropicaltrailrides.com

G

Georgia

- appalachiantrailrides.com
- rideredgate.com
- serenbetrailriding.com
- www.dillardhousestables.com
- rooseveltstablesfdr.com
- www.sunnyfarmsnorth.com
- www.goldcitycorral.com
- www.chattahoocheestables.com
- sunburststables.com
- bluebirdhorsebackriding.com

H

Hawaii

- oahuhorsebackrides.com
- happytrailshawaii.com
- www.panioloadventures.com
- gunstockranch.com
- ironwoodranch.com
- www.silverfallsranch.com
- www.cjmstables.com
- www.mendesranch.com
- waipioonhorseback.com
- ohikilolo.com
- www.makenastables.com

I

Idaho

- http://bit.ly/horse-tours
  mysticsaddleranch.com

- idahoguestranch.com
- www.yellowstoneworld.com
- www.dryridge.com
- www.wbsadventures.com
- saddleupkids.com
- www.dryridge.com
- mountainhorseadventures.com
- mysticsaddleranch.com
- junipermountainoutfitters.com
- westernpleasureranch.com
- www.galenalodge.com

Illinois

- millbrooktrailrides.com
- www.rockinptrails.com
- sarahsponyrides.com
- www.graftontrailrides.com
- royalerancharabianhorses.com
- www.fitzjoyfarm.com
- thegalenaterritory.com
- www.lakeglendalestables.com
- www.fvfarms.com
- www.memorylanestables.com
- lazybequineservices.com
- www.coyotecreektack.com
- www.autumnridgeacres.com

Indiana

- www.ktrails.com
- www.crookedcreekhorsebackriding.com
- grandpajeffshorserides.com
- schoonervalleystables.com
- www.browncounty-saddlebarn.com
- hendrickscountytrailrides.com
- www.wildcatcreekhorsepark.com
- www.shiloranchhobart.com
- web.facebook.com/Shangri-la-800133606694884
- www.santas-stables.com
- www.frenchlick.com/activities/outdoor/stables

- bestrideever.net

K

Kansas

- http://bit.ly/horse-tours
- www.ssstables.com
- www.c-arrow-stables.com
- www.lazybucksranch.com
- www.gypsumhillstrailrides.com
- www.wildroseequinecenter.com
- stormcreekhorseco.business.site
- www.topekaroundupclub.com
- www.flinthillsflyingw.com
- www.yourequineadventure.com/home.html
- www.sunsettrailsstables.com
- www.classictangostables.com/index.html

Kentucky

- whisperingwoodstrails.com
- www.whispervalleytrails.com
- www.bigredstablesky.com
- web.facebook.com/pages/Frick-Farm-Horse-Rescue-and-Trail-Riding/379117352280682?_rdc=1&_rdr
- www.kentuckybyhorse.com
- www.longctrails.com
- www.shelbytrailspark.com
- kentuckyactionpark.com
- web.facebook.com/CumberlandFallsRidingStables
- doublejstables.com/index.htm
- cedarridgefarm.wixsite.com/horses
- kyhorsepark.com

L

Louisiana

- sunflowerfarmandranch.net
- www.hayesedaze.com
- rusticskyhorsecamp.com
- st-john-ranch-louisiana.business.site
- fraziershomestead.com
- splendorfarms.net
- www.sweetwater-campground.com
- www.brec.org/index.cfm/park/FarrPark
- web.facebook.com/pg/Sunny-Slope-Stables-LLC-324043337783708
- www.circlephorseranch.com
- www.cascadestables.net

M

Maine

- http://bit.ly/horse-tours
- www.rosewoodtrailriding.com
- chfmaine.com
- www.deepwoodfarm.com
- livingwellsfarm.com
- www.sableoakec.com
- web.facebook.comCedarWinds Stable
- www.eastmarkfarm.com
- pinelandfarms.org
- www.rangeleyenvironmental.com/index.html
- www.memorylanevacations.net
- www.cottonwoodcampingrvpark.com

Maryland

- www.happyonhooves.com
- www.fairhillstablesllc.com
- hoofprintstrailriding.com
- piscatawaystable.com
- www.fairwindsstables.com
- www.hollyridgefarm.com
- www.westerntrails.net
- www.mistymanor.com
- www.deepcreeklakestable.com
- rosarystables.com
- countrycomfortfarm.com

Massachusetts

- http://bit.ly/horse-tours
- bobbysranch.com
- ridgevalleystables.com
- ponypartyride.com
- www.CornerstoneRanch.org
- www.powderlymeadows.com
- www.hiddenhollowstable.com
- www.churchillstablesma.com
- www.equineblvd.horse
- www.cinchemupstables.com
- undermountainfarm.com
- www.rhapsodyhillfarm.com
- web.facebook.com/A-J-Stables-116652578395158
- www.cantonequestrian.com

Michigan

- www.mayburyridingstable.com
- www.outriderhorsebackriding.com
- 4horserides.com
- pineriverstables.com
- doublejj.com
- stonylakestables.com
- www.cindysridingstable.com
- brightonrecridingstable.com
- www.mapleridgestables.com
- www.laytonsrvf.com
- sundanceridingstable.com

Minnesota

- hopehorseparkclark.wixsite.com
- bunkerparkstable.com
- rivervalleyhorseranch.com
- www.pineriverstable.com
- www.outbackranch.com
- www.horseplayranchmn.com
- sunnysidestables.org
- circlerranch.com
- www.outbackranch.net
- rockislandranch.com
- www.barlstable.com
- www.lucelinestable.com

Mississippi

- rockingmfarm.webs.com
- web.facebook.com/pages/Rock-Hill-Stables/142553292456923?_rdc=1&_rdr
- www.raintreeequestrian.com
- web.facebook.com/pg/altitudetrailrides/about/?ref=page_internal
- www.circlehranchfoxtrotters.comindex.html

Missouri

- goldenhills.com
- web.facebook.com/Old-Family-Farm-Trail-Rides-1523079891237249
- www.thouvenelstables.com
- www.sunsettrailsstables.com
- free.facebook.com/bearcreektrailrides/about/?refid=17
- www.brushycreeklodge.com
- www.cedaridgetrails.com
- eagle-ranch.com

- trailrides.krausfarms.com
- rockingj.com
- web.facebook.com/Aceridingstable
- www.wildroseequinecenter.com
- www.saddlecreekhorses.net

Montana

- http://bit.ly/horse-tours maeramontana.org
- paintbrushadventures.com
- elkriveradventures.com
- bittercreekoutfitters.com
- www.hidalgotrailrides.com
- jakeshorses.com/index.html
- www.swanmountainoutfitters.com
- www.swanmountainglacier.com
- www.yellowstonepacktrips.com index.html
- jmbaroutfitters.com
- thediamondpranch.com
- cachecreekoutfitters.com

N

Nebraska

- countrytrailstables.com
- www.shadylaneranch.com
- miraclehillsranch.com
- visitfreemanscorner.com
- www.logbarnstables.com
- www.dustytrails.biz
- www.mountainrosehorsemanship.com
- www.lazykarena.comdefault.htm

Nevada

- www.cowboytrailrides.com
- www.wildwesthorsebackadventures.com
- ranchoredrock.com
- silverstatetour.com
- www.pipingrockhorses.com
- www.sheridancreekequestriancenter.com
- web.facebook.com/crossjkranch
- kylecanyonhorsestable.com
- www.happyhoofbeats.com
- tahoerimtrail.org
- www.zephyrcovestable.com

New Hampshire

- www.lucky7stables.com
- www.ridingintheclouds.comindex.html
- franconianotchstables.com
- www.highmeadowsfarms.com
- www.shannontrails.com
- www.northroadfarm.com
- thelazyponyfarm.com
- www.wingedspurfarm.com
- www.highknollequestrian.com
- coldbrookfarmnh.com
- jarahsustinstables.com
- www.hollisranch.com

New Jersey

- www.legacyridingstables.com
- www.serenehorseranch.com
- www.topviewridingranch.com
- www.eliteequinegroup.com
- www.splitelm.com
- www.echolakestables.com
- www.handyacresnj.com
- www.mortonhousefarm.com
- www.seatonhackney.com
- www.ddstables.com
- www.somersetcountyparks.org

New Mexico

- http://bit.ly/horse-tours
  www.runninghorseranchabq.com
- acaciaridingadventures.com
- www.cedarcreststables.com
- www.brokensaddle.com
- utrail.com
- acaciaridingadventures.com
- www.visionquesthorsebackrides.com
- www.enchantmentequitreks.com
- www.riograndestables.net
- www.redriverstables.com
- elpasotrailrides.com
- geronimoranch.com/

New York

- kensingtonstables.com
- www.westchestertrailrides.com
- www.babylonridingcenterny.com
- www.bigriverbarn.com
- www.juckasstables.com
- www.foxhillfarms.net
- nativity-riding-academy.com
- www.mynyec.com
- www.nycgovparks.org
- www.cimarronranchny.net
- www.skybluestables.com

North Carolina

- www.sandybottomtrailrides.net
- www.vx3trailrides.com
- www.smokymountaintrailrides.com
- www.dutchcreektrails.com
- www.saddleuptrailrides.com
- www.deadbrokefarm.com
- horsebacktrailriding.com
- chunkygalstables.com

- www.smokemontridingstable.com

North Dakota

- medora.com/do/outdoor/medora-riding-stables-trail-rides
- dustytrailriders.org/index.html
- www.bismarckhorseclub.com?id=4

O

Ohio

- www.amishcountryridingstables.com
- www.marmonvalleyhorsefarm.com
- benshappytrails.com
- www.thespottedhorseranch.com
- www.unclebucksstable.com
- www.eastforkstables.net
- www.foundtreasures77.com
- www.bluemoonacresstable.com
- royalcreekfarm.com
- www.knoxcountyhorsepark.com
- www.equestrianvalley.com
- www.saltforkstables.com
- www.faithranch.org

Oklahoma

- equiadventures.com
- www.honeyleeranchok.com
- www.silverwindstables.com
- arbuckletrailrides.com
- oldcaldwelltrail.com
- www.lakesidetrailride.com

- robberscavestables.com
- rivermantrailrides.com
- www.lakeeufaula.com/news--outdoors--Arrowhead-Riding-Stables-At-Lake-Eufaula-Ok/4761
- chickasawcountry.com/family-attractions/lake-murray-riding-stables

Oregon

- www.dreamridgestable.com
- www.centraloregontrailrides.com
- smithrocktrailrides.com
- www.oregonbeachrides.com
- www.ridinginhoodriver.com
- www.perrydaletrails.com
- blackbuttestables.com
- www.bendhorseride.com
- www.fiddlestixranch.com
- diamondlakecorrals.com
- skyranchstables.com
- www.junipertrails.com

P

Pennsylvania

- http://bit.ly/horse-tours
- mtcreekstable.com
- www.hickoryhollowfarm.com
- confederatetrails.com
- haycockstables.com
- www.redbuffaloranch.com
- nittanymountaintrailrides.com
- www.patrailride.com
- smfhorses.com
- www.deerpathstable.com

R

Rhode Island

- sunsetstablesri.com
- web.facebook.com/rusticrideshorsefarm
- www.newportequestrian.com
- gracenotefarmweb.com
- enshantingalliestables.weebly.com

S

South Carolina

- www.lakeviewplantation.com
- myrtlebeachhorserides.com
- www.seahorseaiken.com
- www.grandstrandhorsebackriding.com
- www.daufuskietrailrides.com
- www.blackhorserunsc.net
- wampeestables.com
- www.inletpointplantation.com
- www.middletonplaceequestriancenter.com
- redbarnriding.com
- www.edenfarms.net
- bluewavestable.com

South Dakota

- www.andystrailrides.com
- www.rockingrtrailrides.com
- ridesouthdakota.com
- tandmtrailrides.com
- www.sagemeadowranchllc.com
- www.rrrranch.com

T

Tennessee

- http://bit.ly/horse-tours
- www.longctrails.com
- nashvillehorsebackriding.com
- www.sugarlandsridingstables.com
- www.southeastpacktrips.com
- www.jurostables.com
- www.adventureparkatfiveoaks.com
- horseridingbigrock.com
- www.cadescovestables.com
- lakemeadowfarm.com
- www.fallcreekfallsridingstables.com
- creeksideridingstables.com
- www.ocoeehorseride.com
- www.jayellranch.com

Texas

- http://bit.ly/horse-tours
- www.texastrailrides.com
- strickertrailrides.com
- maverickhorsebackriding.com
- dallashorseback.com
- cypresstrailsranch.com
- www.chisholmtrailrides.com
- westcreektrailrides.com
- brazosbluffsstables.com
- travisptrailrides.net
- juniperhillstables.com
- marshallcreekranch.com

U

Utah

- ziontrailrides.com
- www.thisistheplace.org
- www.canyonrides.com
- www.kbhorses.com
- www.horserides.net
- www.hondoo.com
- www.snowcanyontrailrides.com
- www.risingkranchtrailrides.com
- northfortyescapes.com
- www.rockymtnoutfitters.com
- web.facebook.com/winterhawktrailrides/?_rdc=1&_rdr
- www.redrockride.com/

V

Vermont

- http://bit.ly/horse-tours
- lajoiestables.com
- www.chipmanstables.com
- www.breakaway-farm.com
- mountainviewranch.biz
- icelandichorses.com
- kimberlyfarms.org
- www.pondhillranch.com
- www.ahasohillfarm.com
- www.brooksidestables.com
- www.upnorthstables.com
- www.centerforamericasfirsthorse.org

Virginia

- www.marriottranch.com
- www.fortvalleystable.com
- northmtnoutfitter.com
- www.lakewoodtrailrides.com
- www.appalachianhorseadventures.org
- www.beaverhollowfarm.com
- magicmountainfarm.com
- slocumshorsebackriding.com
- www.shangrilaguestranch.com

W

Washington

- http://bit.ly/horse-tours
- www.eztimeshorserides.com
- misty-acres-ravensdale-wa.weebly.com
- www.equineescapes.com
- www.petsgalorehorserides.com
- www.wildathearthorserides.com
- www.redmountaintrails.com
- kinshiptrailrides.com
- www.horsecountryfarm.com
- www.orcastrailrides.com
- spokanetrailrides.com
- www.3peaksoutfitters.com
- www.sudarariding.net

West Virginia

- www.mountaintrailrides.com
- www.horseshoecreekridingstable.com

- www.hiddentrailsstableswv.com
- www.yokums-stables.biz
- www.horsebackwv.com
- oglebay.com
- web.facebook.com/MajesticReinsStableLlc
- magicmountainfarm.com
- www.tsaheylufarm.com
- www.ejcottages.net

Wisconsin

- dreamahorse.com
- www.bighorn1ranch.com
- redrocktrailrides.com
- www.wild3lranch.com
- www.appyorseacres.com
- www.kettlemoraineranch.com
- www.wildernesspursuit.com
- www.spiderlakeranch.com
- westerntrailsequestrian.com
- www.redridgeranch.com
- www.hoofbeatridge.com
- web.facebook.comLeeLakeRidingStables?_rdc=1&_rdr

Wyoming

- http://bit.ly/horse-tours
- www.fishjacksonwyo.com
- www.codyyellowstone.org
- rockinmranchwyoming.com
- www.grbto.com
- www.millironranch.net
- wyomingsummerpacktrips.com
- www.horsebackadv.com
- billcodyranch.com
- www.yellowstone.ws
- www.lazylb.com
- rockinmhorsebackrides.com

Worldwide Travel Agencies Index

Resources for Equestrians

Below is a list of other helpful resources available for FREE on the Equestrian Adventuresses website. In this mega-resource list you will find:

1) Educational Books
2) Packing Lists
3) Long Riding Articles
4) List of 55+ Horse Travel Books
5) Fitness for Equestrians List
6) Riding Tips
7) Long Riding tips
8) Travel Advice
9) Destination Guides

And much, much more!

Click here or visit the website:
https:catalog.equestrianadventuresses.com/resources

Job Listings

GREECE

Horseland - VOLUNTEER POSITIONS AVAILABLE, please email for more information on the exchange offered. mykonoshorseland@hotmail.com

EGYPT

Equestrian Dream Egypt - We are looking for a groom/rider/guide to complete our team. We are looking for candidates with experience in handling young horses ,with a good sense of responsibility, the ability to work in a team, and to deal with customers. Our stable is located in the desert of Hurghada and is designed for the well-being of our horses, which are all rescued from terrible situations. Our activities range from riding lessons to excursions in the desert (from 1 hour or even more days)
www.equestriandreamegypt.com
info@equestriandreamegypt.com

PERU

Hacienda del Chalán - An amazing experience on our small family Ranch in the Sacred Valley of the Incas. We offer horseback riding tours along the Peruvian Andes. As a volunteer couple you will help out (25 hrs per week) with feeding the animals, cleaning and handy work around the stables, saddling the horses, equine therapy and house holding tasks. We offer an all-in stay at our Ranch, possibility to join the riding tours and free time to discover the culture/nature.
www.haciendadelchalan.com
reservas@haciendadelchalan.com

NEW MEXICO, USA

Enchantment Equitreks - SHARE OUR MISSION: Our core mission to rehabilitate and rehome rescue horses is the focal point of our business and we want to share our experiences with you. This 8 day working vacation program offers riders age 15 and older the ability to develop their trail riding skills, learn to work with rescue horses, and immerse themselves in the Southwest culture. Each day will be spent working on the ranch, in the saddle, and engaging with clients. Down time can be spent at the pool or hot tub, hiking, biking, or joining a yoga class.

http://www.enchantmentequitreks.com/trail-rides#working-vacation

AFRICAN HORSE SAFARIS WORKING HOLIDAYS

MOZAMBIQUE

Trail Riding Volunteer in Tropical Paradise

Work with horses in tropical paradise. Explore white sand beaches and warm Indian Ocean. Hone your riding skills on the warm beaches, assist trail riding guests and learn about horse care at a stud. Stay 2 – 12 weeks. Cost from USD1 700 for 2 weeks

https://africanhorsesafaris.com/riding-focuses/volunteer-horses/

isabel@africanhorsesafaris.com

SOUTH AFRICA

Holistic horsemanship Volunteer

Care for string of athletic, fit-trail horses while learning about the yard's ethos of holistic horsemanship. Endless beach gallops, authentic Wild Coast experience, unique coastal landscape. Stay 2-12 weeks. Cost from USD1 500 for 2 weeks

https://africanhorsesafaris.com/riding-focuses/volunteer-horses/

isabel@africanhorsesafaris.com

Riding and Wildlife focused Working Holiday

Volunteer near the world-famous Kruger National Park. Daily life includes jumping lessons, dressage lessons, trail riding with wildlife, horseback swims, basic veterinary skills, yard management and wildlife conservation. Ride daily and live in a Big 5 reserve with unique African wildlife. Stay 2 – 12 weeks. Cost from USD1 100 for 2 weeks

https://africanhorsesafaris.com/riding-focuses/volunteer-horses/

isabel@africanhorsesafaris.com

ZIMBABWE

Wildlife and Riding Working Holiday in Zimbabwe

Volunteer at this safari lodge where you may have daily interaction with the resident elephant and other wildlife. Receive hands-on experience in stable management, riding lessons, basic veterinary and trail riding with guests. Ride with plains game, swim with horses, take giraffe selfies, try Polocrosse and visit the Victoria Falls. Stay 2 – 12 weeks. Cost from USD1 575 for 2 weeks

https://africanhorsesafaris.com/riding-focuses/volunteer-horses/

isabel@africanhorsesafaris.com

About
Equestrian Adventuresses

Equestrian Adventuresses was founded in 2019 as a community for women who love horses, travel and adventure.

You can listen to more inspirational stories from real women's travels on horseback on the podcast show available on iTunes, Spotify, Stitcher and more. http:bit.ly/eqa-podcast

You can also find a variety of travel documentaries on the Youtube Channel:
www.youtube.com/c/equestrianadventuresses

You can also read short stories and find helpful resources on the website:
www.equestrianadventuresses.com

Join the community and check out the Facebook Group:
https:www.facebook.com/groups/equestrianadventuresses

Other Books By Equestrian Adventuresses:

EQUESTRIAN ADVENTURESSES SERIES

Book 1: Saddles and Sisterhood
Book 2: Going the Distance
Book 3: Leg Up
Book 4: Have Breeches Will Travel
Book 5: Horse Nomads

TRAVEL GUIDE FOR EQUESTRIANS SERIES

Best in 2020 World Travel Guide
Best in 2020 USA Travel Guide
2021 Job Book - How to Work Abroad with Horses
Horse Riding in Every Country: A Catalog of Riding
Opportunities in Over 180+ Countries

*Download your FREE E-Book here:
www.EquestrianAdventuresses.com

Coming Soon!

Around the World on 180 Horses Series
Fairy Tail

*Books are available on Amazon, Audible, Kobo and more!
You can also find them on our website:
www.equestrianadventuresses.com

Dreaming of Traveling the World on Horseback but Don't Know Where to Start?

Introducing the **Equestrian Adventuresses Online Courses,** the first ever online home-study courses that gives you the necessary confidence and skills to become an equestrian adventuress.

What you'll learn:
- How to Speak the Horse Language in ANY country
- How to be more confident on the ground and in the saddle with horses
- How to travel solo confidently
- Develop a "Sticky Butt" in the saddle
- How to gain your horse's trust and build their confidence
- Mastering your own body language
- What is "Energy" and how does it influence your horse
- How to stay safe while traveling as a solo woman
- How to read situations
- Effective strategies to turn your goals, ideas & dreams into ACTIONABLE PLANS
- And much, much more!

For more information check out the Equestrian Adventuresses Online Courses Here:
www.EquestrianAdventuresses.com

Thank You For Reading!

Dear Reader,

I hope you enjoyed this 4th installment in the Equestrian Adventuresses Travel Guide Book Series. I have to tell you, this has been a pleasure being able to make the world of horseback travel accessible to all. If you crave stories of women's true encounters with horse nomadism and long riding, fear not, you can read their inspiring stories in our Equestrian Adventuresses Book Series. As an author, I love feedback. I have received many messages from readers thanking me for this series for inspiring them to travel on horseback and take a chance.

You are the reason I will continue to research and provide valuable information. Please let us know what you liked, loved and even what you hated. I'd love to hear from you. You can email me at www.equestrianadventuresses.com or post in our Facebook Group.

I need to ask a favor. If your so inclined, I'd love it if you would post a review on Amazon. Loved it, hated it—I'd just like to hear your feedback. Reviews can be tough to come by these days, and you, the reader, have the power to make or break a book. If you have the time, here's a link to my author page, along with all my books on amazon: **www.amazon.com/author/krystal-kelly**

Thank you so much for downloading this book and for spending time with me. I look forward to many more adventures together in the future!

In Gratitude,
Krystal Kelly
Equestrian Adventuresses Founder

Printed in France by Amazon
Brétigny-sur-Orge, FR

14050133R00098